Evaluate to Elevate

Rethinking Performance Evaluation in the Public Sector

Dr. Patrick C. Patrong

President/CEO
Patrong Enterprises, Inc.

Richmond, VA

Evaluate to Elevate: Rethinking Performance Evaluation in the Public Sector

For information regarding permissions or speaking engagements, contact:
Patrong Enterprises, Inc.

Richmond, Virginia
Website: www.patrong.com

Telephone/WhatsApp: 1.410.294.5431
Email: info@patrong.com

All examples, case studies, and scenarios in this book are inspired by real organizational settings but are presented in a composite form to preserve confidentiality and learning value. Names, roles, and details have been altered to protect confidentiality.

Printed in the United States of America.

ISBN: 979-8-9998411-0-0

Library of Congress Control Number: *Pending*

Design and Layout: Patrong Enterprises, Inc. **Cover Design:** "PEI Creative Studio 1A

First Edition: 2025

Legal Disclaimer
This publication is intended to provide general leadership and supervisory guidance. It is not intended to substitute for legal, human resources, or compliance advice tailored to any specific organization. Readers should consult their agency or legal counsel before applying any policies or procedures discussed in this book.

Acknowledgments

This book represents more than a professional milestone—it reflects a shared belief in the transformative power of leadership that listens, evaluates, and elevates. I am deeply grateful to the many colleagues, mentors, and public servants who have shaped my understanding of what effective leadership looks like in practice.

To my colleagues at the Virginia Museum of Fine Arts, thank you for demonstrating that purpose and professionalism can coexist beautifully. Your dedication to growth, accountability, and collaboration inspired many of the real-world examples throughout these pages.

To the public sector leaders across state and local agencies who have allowed me to teach, learn, and grow alongside you, your courage to lead with integrity continues to remind me why this work is so important.

To the students, mentees, and participants in countless leadership sessions, your questions, reflections, and willingness to evolve have given life to the concepts in this book.

To my family, whose patience, love, and unwavering encouragement sustain me—you remind me that leadership begins at home.

Finally, to every supervisor who believes that evaluation is not about judgment but about development—this book was written for you. May it help you see that feedback is not an obligation but a privilege that has the power to change lives.

Preface

When I began my career in public service, I quickly realized that evaluation—one of the most critical leadership tools—was often misunderstood, avoided, or reduced to a yearly formality. Supervisors filled out checkboxes. Employees waited anxiously for ratings. The process was mechanical, not meaningful.

Over the years, I have seen the cost of neglect and the potential when it's done right. When evaluation turns into conversation, and conversation turns into culture, organizations change. Performance improves not through pressure but through partnership. Trust grows when leaders provide feedback with honesty, consistency, and care.

Evaluate to Elevate was written to restore that sense of purpose. It invites supervisors to view evaluation not as a human resources task, but as a daily act of leadership. Each chapter is designed to provide both structure and a strategic blend of practical tools and philosophical grounding. Readers will find real public-sector examples, reflection questions, and evidence-based approaches that make evaluation accessible, equitable, and inspiring.

This is not a book about forms. It is a book about people—their growth, contributions, and potential. It challenges every supervisor to see evaluation as both a mirror and a map: a reflection of leadership values and a guide for developing others.

As you read, I encourage you to consider not only how you evaluate, but why. Because in the end, evaluation done well does more than measure performance, it elevates culture.

— Dr. Patrick C. Patrong

Contents

Rethinking Evaluation in the Public Sector

Performance evaluation remains one of the most underutilized tools in public sector leadership. Too often, supervisors view evaluations as bureaucratic necessities—checklists that must be completed annually to satisfy HR policies. This mindset results in missed opportunities to coach employees, recognize excellence, correct course, or align individual contributions with broader agency goals.

This chapter reframes evaluation as a core leadership practice, not just a process. It is written for new and seasoned supervisors who may not have received formal training in performance evaluation, and it aims to reintroduce evaluation as a high-impact, developmental, and strategic tool within your leadership toolkit.

What You Will Learn

- Understand the strategic purpose of evaluation beyond compliance.

- Identify common myths and challenges that hinder effective evaluations in the public sector.

- Discover how transitioning to a development-centered model can enhance organizational culture.

The Strategic Purpose of Evaluation

At its core, performance evaluation in the public sector is about more than rating performance—it is about clarifying expectations, aligning efforts, and building a high-functioning workforce. In environments where accountability to citizens, ethical standards, and stewardship of public resources are paramount, supervisors must elevate the way they assess, guide, and support their teams. Evaluations serve as the medium through which leaders translate agency priorities into everyday performance, helping individuals understand the broader value of their work.

Supervisors often overlook the communication power embedded in evaluations. A well-conducted evaluation is a strategic message to employees: You are seen. Your work matters. Your development is part of our future. When evaluations are taken seriously and tied to larger agency goals—such as improving citizen service, achieving budget targets, or enhancing community trust—they elevate the connection between individual performance and the organizational mission.

The strategic purpose of evaluation also lies in its ability to create focus. With numerous competing demands in public service roles, employees often require clarity on what truly matters. Evaluation cycles provide the structure for conversations about goals, success metrics, and developmental pathways. It helps employees prioritize tasks that align with agency objectives and avoid spending time on activities that are low-impact or misaligned with these objectives.

Furthermore, evaluations serve as a developmental mirror. They offer space to affirm strengths, acknowledge areas of growth, and outline the support employees need to advance. When supervisors use evaluations to ask questions, "What do you need from me to succeed?" or "What are your long-term professional goals?"—they unlock employee potential and build trust. The process becomes not just evaluative, but collaborative, reinforcing the shared responsibility between supervisor and employee.

In summary, the strategic purpose of evaluation lies in its ability to align individual action with organizational mission, provide clarity and focus, and offer a platform for growth. When approached with intention, evaluation becomes more than documentation—it becomes a declaration of leadership.

Common Myths and Missed Opportunities

Despite its importance, performance evaluations are surrounded by persistent myths that undermine their effectiveness. One of the most harmful is the belief that evaluations are only necessary when performance is poor. This belief causes supervisors to put off evaluations or engage in minimal effort unless there is a problem to address. Every employee benefits from evaluation—whether they are high performers, steady contributors, or in need of growth.

Another common myth is that evaluations must be vague or overly optimistic to avoid conflict. Many supervisors fear the consequences of honesty—afraid that a less-than-perfect rating will damage morale or invite pushback. As a result, they default to middle-of-the-road ratings, avoid clear feedback, and create confusion for the employee. The result? Underperformers feel secure, while top performers feel unseen.

A third myth is the idea that evaluations are isolated events, disconnected from the rest of the year. When evaluations are treated as annual tasks, they lose their power to influence behavior. Feedback is most effective when it is consistent, timely, and tied to specific examples. When supervisors rely solely on memory or incomplete records, they risk falling into bias or making judgments based on the most recent event—what we call the Flash Effect.

These myths also represent a significant missed opportunity: the chance to utilize evaluations as a retention and engagement strategy. Employees who feel overlooked or underappreciated are more likely to disengage or leave their organization. Performance evaluations offer a structured opportunity to recognize contributions, coach employees through challenges, and affirm their commitment to growth. It is an investment that pays off in loyalty and performance.

To overcome these myths, supervisors must reframe their thinking. Evaluation is not about judgment—it is about partnership. It is not about fault—it is about growth. When viewed through this lens, evaluations become a powerful platform for connection, clarity, and continuous improvement.

Shifting from Compliance to Development

In many public sector agencies, performance evaluation is still primarily driven by compliance—checking boxes, meeting deadlines, and completing required forms. While accountability to policy is essential, a compliance-driven mindset limits the potential of evaluations to develop talent and elevate organizational culture. When evaluations are rushed, vague, or handled solely to meet HR requirements, they fail to create a meaningful impact. Shifting from compliance to development means reclaiming performance evaluation as a leadership responsibility and a tool for employee empowerment.

A development-centered approach to evaluation focuses on long-term growth, not just short-term metrics. Supervisors using this approach consider not only what was achieved, but how it was achieved, and what comes next. They ask questions like, "What skills should this employee develop in the coming year?" What leadership potential are we nurturing? What barriers must be removed to help this individual thrive? These questions promote a mindset of forward-thinking leadership and investment in the future of the workforce.

To adopt a development mindset, supervisors must engage in ongoing dialogue throughout the year. Evaluation is not a one-time event—it is a cycle of feedback, reflection, and realignment. Quarterly check-ins, performance notes, and two-way coaching conversations build the foundation for a more complete, fair, and supportive year-end evaluation. When feedback becomes part of the routine culture, evaluation becomes less threatening and more effective.

Another shift involves how success is defined. In a compliance model, success is measured by whether the form was completed and submitted. In a development model, success is measured by whether the employee understands their feedback, knows how to act on it, and has a growth plan. This approach helps employees feel that they are not being evaluated solely to satisfy bureaucratic requirements—but to enhance their capabilities and contribute more effectively to the agency's mission.

Ultimately, moving from compliance to development transforms the supervisor's role from evaluator to coach. It turns the evaluation process from a transaction into a relationship. When employees sense that their growth is truly valued—not just documented—they engage more deeply. They ask for feedback, take initiative, and bring their best selves to work. The result is a more responsive, resilient, and mission-driven public service workforce.

Summary

This chapter laid the foundation for reimagining performance evaluation in the public sector as a strategic leadership function. By exploring the true purpose of evaluation, we established its role in aligning individual contributions with agency goals and reinforcing employee development. We examined the myths that prevent supervisors from conducting effective evaluations and the missed opportunities that result when evaluation is approached as mere compliance. Ultimately, we emphasized the transformative power of shifting from a compliance-based to a development-focused model—one that fosters ongoing dialogue, drives growth, and cultivates a culture of accountability. Performance evaluation is not simply a form to complete; it is a platform to elevate individuals and organizations. When used intentionally, it can shape culture, enhance engagement, and foster talent development.

In Practice: Public Sector Case Snapshot

Rosa, a supervisor at a state revenue agency, led a team of six administrative specialists. One team member, Calvin, was known for his accuracy, efficiency, and willingness to help others. For three consecutive years, Rosa marked Calvin as "meets expectations" on his evaluation. She believed this was fair—he did everything right, but "did not go beyond."

Calvin quietly applied for another role in a neighboring agency. In his exit interview, he shared that he felt invisible. "I have never had a real conversation about my performance," he said. "Just a form." Rosa was stunned. She had not realized that failing to differentiate performance had signaled that excellence was not recognized or rewarded. The agency lost a high performer not due to pay, but due to disengagement.

The lesson? Recognition and growth feedback are not optional. In a public sector context, where raises and promotions may be limited, well-delivered evaluations become a primary motivator and retention tool.

Reflection Questions

- Have I ever avoided honest feedback because I was afraid of the conversation?

- Do I use the evaluation process to recognize and retain high performers?

- How would my team describe the value or purpose of our evaluation conversations?

- Do I document performance throughout the year, or rely only on memory?

- What is one way I could shift from compliance to development in my next review cycle?

In Practice: Key Takeaways

- Performance evaluation is not just a rating—it is a reflection of your leadership. It communicates what you value and sets the tone for growth.

- Avoiding difficult feedback erodes accountability; avoiding positive feedback erodes engagement.

- Development-focused evaluation involves ongoing conversations, not just end-of-year paperwork.

- Differentiating performance is not only fair—it is necessary to foster excellence and retention.

- Public sector constraints (tenure, compensation, bureaucracy) make meaningful evaluations more critical—not less.

Leadership-Centered Summary

Leadership in the public sector is a daily act of stewardship. Supervisors are not only responsible for getting the work done—they are responsible for shaping the people who do the job. Performance evaluation is one of the few formal, recurring opportunities a leader has to pause the chaos, offer clarity, and invest in growth. When this moment is treated as a checkbox, the workforce stagnates. However, when it is approached as a moment of truth, it becomes a lever for excellence.

The way you evaluate your team speaks volumes about the culture you are creating. Do you value effort or only outcomes? Do you correct quietly or coach deliberately? Do your employees leave evaluations with clarity, or with questions? These are the leadership questions that define not just your supervisory style, but your legacy.

Remember: your evaluation is not just a form. It is a statement of belief. It tells your team whether you see them, support them, and believe in their potential to grow. It sets the tone for the conversations you are willing to have and the culture you are building day by day. When done well, evaluation is not just retrospective—it is visionary.

Furthermore, it is needed now more than ever. In an era of shrinking budgets, growing demands, and public scrutiny, our ability to build high-performing, mission-driven teams will depend on our willingness to evaluate with candor and care.

"Evaluation done right is not about checking boxes—it is about lighting beacons. Each one signals value, direction, and belief in what is possible.
— *Dr. Patrick C. Patrong*

The Five-Point Performance Scale Explained

One of the most common challenges supervisors face in the public sector is distinguishing between levels of performance. Without a clear framework, supervisors may default to vague or middling evaluations—undermining the value of the review itself. In this chapter, we introduce the five-point performance scale used throughout this guide and explain how it empowers supervisors to rate fairly, communicate clearly, and lead with credibility. Each level of the scale represents more than a rating—it represents a pattern of behavior, contribution, and commitment to the agency's mission. You will learn not only what each level means, but how to recognize and apply them consistently.

What You Will Learn

- Understand the purpose and structure of a five-point performance rating system.

- Distinguish clearly between Extraordinary, Highly Successful, Successful, Partially Successful, and Unsuccessful performance.

- Apply behavioral anchors and examples to improve evaluation accuracy and credibility.

Extraordinary

Extraordinary performance is rare, but unmistakable. These employees do more than their job—they redefine how their job adds value to the agency. They show initiative, leadership, and impact that far exceeds expectations. Their contributions ripple beyond their individual assignments to uplift teams, improve systems, and advance the mission. They innovate, coach others, and drive results without waiting to be asked.

In the public sector, where roles are often rigid and processes entrenched, extraordinary employees bring flexibility and foresight. They anticipate needs before others recognize them. Their work is timely, accurate, and strategically aligned. They are not just reliable—they are catalytic.

Supervisors should recognize extraordinary performers not only through ratings, but also by providing them with visibility and opportunities for growth. Failing to do so risks disengagement or departure. These individuals are often seen as culture carriers—setting the tone for what is possible.

It is important not to confuse likability or tenure with extraordinary performance. This rating is reserved for those who change outcomes, elevate standards, and build capacity across the organization. Their influence is broad and deep.

Employees who meet the extraordinary standard should leave the evaluation conversation energized, valued, and ready to lead. They are your future trainers, mentors, and internal change agents.

Highly Successful

Highly successful employees are dependable, consistent, and often proactive. They regularly exceed expectations in key areas and bring additional value to their role. Unlike extraordinary performers who transform systems, highly successful employees improve them within scope. They are the backbone of high-performing teams.

In public sector environments, highly successful employees deliver with minimal supervision and often support colleagues. They suggest improvements, handle assignments with initiative, and demonstrate pride in their work. They may not lead significant change efforts, but their presence elevates quality and continuity.

Supervisors must be careful not to overlook these employees. While not flashy, their steady performance allows agencies to meet service goals and build trust. They deserve more than a standard "thank you"—they deserve an explicit acknowledgment.

Highly successful performers often transition into supervisory roles or become subject matter experts over time. Their evaluation conversation should include a discussion of developmental opportunities and pathways to broader impact.

Recognizing a highly successful performer keeps them engaged and shows the team that consistent, high-quality work is valued and rewarded—even in the absence of dramatic success stories.

Successful

A successful employee meets expectations reliably. Their work is consistent, accurate, and aligned with their job description. They contribute to the team, follow through on assignments, and demonstrate professionalism.

In public sector teams, successful employees play a crucial role in maintaining the organization's baseline. They fulfill responsibilities without regular reminders and require only standard oversight. They are dependable and trusted to deliver their promises.

While this is a positive rating, supervisors should still aim to keep the employee engaged. Complacency can set in if the employee feels unnoticed. Pairing acknowledgment with encouragement to grow helps sustain motivation.

Supervisors should offer concrete examples of what was done well and suggest small stretch goals to prepare for future responsibilities.

Evaluation for successful performers should include positive reinforcement, clarity on what exceeding expectations looks like, and an invitation to contribute in new ways if the employee is interested.

Partially Successful

Partially successful employees meet some, but not all, expectations. They may deliver inconsistently, miss deadlines, or require more supervision than appropriate for their role.

This rating does not necessarily reflect a lack of effort—it may signal gaps in skills, unclear expectations, or new challenges that require further development. Supervisors must determine whether the issue is related to ability, clarity, or accountability.

A partially successful rating requires a development plan. The evaluation conversation must be candid and specific. Highlight what is going well and clarify where performance needs to improve.

Avoid generic statements. Use clear examples, and where appropriate, include input from others to support your points. Set measurable expectations for the next cycle.

This rating is not punitive —it is a redirection. When delivered with respect and followed up with support, this feedback can help the employee rebound and thrive.

Unsuccessful

An unsuccessful rating indicates that the employee consistently failed to meet expectations. There were significant performance deficiencies that impacted operations, service, and team morale.

This rating often follows a series of documented interventions, coaching efforts, or performance discussions. If those efforts were not made, supervisors should review the process and consult HR before assigning this rating.

An unsuccessful employee may struggle due to skill gaps, attitude issues, or disengagement from the job. Supervisors must separate performance from personality and ensure feedback is behavior-based.

The evaluation conversation should be direct, specific, and paired with clear next steps. In some cases, this may include a performance improvement plan (PIP), reassignment, or even separation.

This rating requires courage. However, when handled appropriately, it protects standards, reinforces fairness, and signals that the organization takes performance seriously.

In Practice: Public Sector Case Snapshot

Malik, a facilities supervisor in a mid-sized county government, noticed that one of his team members, Trina, always finished assignments on time but never took initiative. She did not cause issues, but neither did she innovate or collaborate. For three years, she received "Successful" ratings. Meanwhile, a newer employee, Ramon, had proposed scheduling changes that saved time and improved service. Malik hesitated to give Ramon a higher rating—he did not want to "cause waves." Ramon was rated as "Successful."

Ramon later confided in HR that he felt discouraged. His ideas had helped the department, but his evaluation did not reflect that. Within six months, he transferred to another department. Malik realized that he had allowed comfort to override clarity—and that failing to differentiate performance had cost the team its most promising contributor.

Reflection Questions

- Do I clearly understand the difference between "Highly Successful" and "Extraordinary" performance?

- Have I ever defaulted to a "Successful" rating to avoid making a difficult call?

- What systems do I have in place to track performance throughout the year?

- Do I use evaluations to recognize growth and potential, or just past behavior?

- How confident am I in defending my rating decisions with specific examples?

In Practice: Key Takeaways

- Clear rating definitions help supervisors evaluate fairly and communicate accurately.

- Distinguishing between levels like "Highly Successful" and "Extraordinary" motivates top performers and prevents talent loss.

- Rating inflation, or "middling," sends the wrong message to high and low performers.

- Public sector evaluation should reflect what was done and how it aligns with mission and impact.

- Documentation, consistency, and courage are essential to applying the five-point scale effectively.

Leadership-Centered Summary

The power of the five-point scale lies not in its structure—but in your courage to use it. As a public sector supervisor, your role is to recognize performance in all its complexity: the steady contributors, the rising stars, and those in need of growth and development. A strong evaluation system helps clarify expectations, reward impact, and uphold fairness across your team. Nevertheless, only when you apply it with honesty, precision, and the leadership it deserves.

Each rating tells a story. Ensure yours reflects the truth—not just what is convenient.

"A rating is not just a number—it is a message. When delivered with courage and clarity, it becomes a mirror, a map, and a motivator."

— Dr. Patrick C. Patrong

Recognizing Bias in Performance Ratings

No matter how well-intentioned, supervisors carry personal perspectives that shape how they evaluate others. These perspectives, if left unchecked, can introduce unconscious bias into performance evaluations, eroding fairness, morale, and trust. In the public sector, where transparency, equity, and credibility are essential, the stakes are exceptionally high. This chapter examines common rating biases that impact supervisors and offers practical strategies to address them. By naming these patterns—such as the Shine Effect, Stain Effect, Middling Mindset, and Flash Effect—leaders can evaluate with clarity and integrity.

What You Will Learn

- Identify common evaluation biases that affect fairness and consistency.

- Understand the causes and consequences of Shine, Stain, Middling, and Flash effects.

- Apply practical strategies to recognize and reduce bias during evaluation discussions.

The Shine Effect

The Shine Effect occurs when a single, standout trait—such as charisma, creativity, or reliability—colors a supervisor's overall view of an employee's performance. This effect leads to inflated evaluations where excellence in one area overshadows critical gaps in others.

In public sector settings, this bias often appears when an employee excels in high-visibility projects or shares traits with the evaluator. While their strength may be genuine, allowing it to define the entire rating distorts the accuracy of performance.

The Shine Effect is especially dangerous because it is easy to rationalize. Supervisors might justify top scores with phrases like, "They always step up," without citing evidence across all required competencies.

To overcome this bias, supervisors must ground evaluations in documented examples and differentiate between traits and results. Using structured rating tools and peer feedback helps strike a balance between admiration and objectivity.

Recognizing the Shine Effect enables supervisors to be generous without being biased—to reward standout traits while upholding well-rounded performance standards.

The Stain Effect

The Stain Effect is the inverse of the Shine Effect. One negative behavior, event, or trait disproportionately influences a supervisor's rating of an employee, even when the rest of their performance is solid.

This effect might occur after a conflict, a missed deadline, or even a poor attitude observed in a stressful moment. The employee is then seen through the lens of that moment, and their accomplishments are minimized or dismissed.

Public sector supervisors must be particularly cautious of this bias, as civil service roles often require just cause for any adverse action. Relying on emotion rather than evidence undermines not only fairness but also the principles of due process.

The best protection against the Stain Effect is consistency. Document accomplishments and setbacks across the year. If one moment still stands out, ask whether it was part of a larger pattern—or an isolated exception.

When handled carefully, confronting this bias can restore employee confidence, improve accountability, and promote a growth mindset across the team.

The Middling Mindset and Flash Effect

The Middling Mindset reflects a common hesitation: rating everyone as "Successful" to avoid discomfort. It has often been driven by a fear of conflict, claims of favoritism, or a simple lack of confidence in using higher or lower ratings.

Over time, this pattern erodes morale. High performers often feel ignored; underperformers, on the other hand, tend to feel secure. The evaluation loses its meaning as a development tool—and becomes a formality.

The Flash Effect, on the other hand, is rooted in recency bias. Supervisors may give more weight to the most recent event—positive or negative—rather than the whole review period.

Patterns are fixable with structure. Calendar reminders for quarterly notes, peer feedback forms, and calibrated review meetings help ground evaluations in the full year of work—not a single month or mood.

Addressing these effects requires courage. Nevertheless, when done well, performance ratings become more transparent, fairer, and more motivating for the entire team.

In Practice: Public Sector Case Snapshot

Jasmine, a supervisor in a large city transportation agency, was preparing evaluations for her operations team. One employee, Aaron, had made a visible mistake during a community meeting, forgetting key details while representing the department. Though his year had been solid—he implemented a new scheduling system and reduced overtime—Jasmine could not shake the embarrassment from that one moment. She rated him as "Partially Successful," noting his "lack of readiness" in high-pressure situations.

During the review, Aaron expressed shock. "That was one day," he said. "But I improved operations for months." Jasmine realized she had fallen into the Stain Effect. She revised the review based on full-year documentation and recalibrated his rating to "Highly Successful." The experience reminded her that memory is not enough—data matters.

Reflection Questions

- Which type of bias—Shine, Stain, Middling, or Flash—am I most susceptible to?

- Have I ever allowed one recent event to influence an entire performance rating?

- Do I avoid using higher or lower ratings to maintain harmony or avoid scrutiny?

- What steps can I take to ensure that my evaluations accurately reflect the full performance cycle?

- How do I create opportunities for peer input or a third-party perspective in ratings?

In Practice: Key Takeaways

- Bias in performance ratings can distort fairness, demotivate staff, and misdirect development.

- Shine and Stain Effects stem from over-reliance on single traits or events.

- The Middling Mindset results from fear of discomfort, often weakening accountability.

- The Flash Effect prioritizes recency over consistency, but this is corrected by documentation.

- Supervisors who reflect, calibrate, and document can avoid bias and lead with integrity.

Evaluating with Awareness and Intentionality

Biases are not character flaws—they are natural tendencies in human judgment. However, when left unchecked, they can erode the credibility and developmental value of performance evaluations. The

Shine Effect, Stain Effect, Middling Mindset, and Flash Effect represent common but avoidable patterns that distort how we assess others. These biases can lead to inflated ratings, overlooked contributions, unfair criticism, or missed opportunities for growth. Recognizing them by name gives supervisors the language and clarity needed to pause, reflect, and correct course during evaluation discussions.

Addressing bias is not about perfection—it is about practice and awareness. When supervisors document performance throughout the cycle, use evidence-based criteria, and engage in honest conversations, evaluations become more than a compliance task—they become catalysts for clarity, accountability, and employee development. The responsibility of rating with fairness and courage rests not just in forms or systems, but in the mindset with which we lead.

Leadership-Centered Summary

Evaluating with fairness requires more than process compliance; it requires personal awareness. Each of us brings past experiences, preferences, and blind spots into performance discussions. As public sector leaders, we must take responsibility for those tendencies and proactively correct them. Bias awareness does not mean being perfect—it means being deliberate.

Supervisors who recognize their bias tendencies and use structured, evidence-based evaluation tools create teams that trust the system—and the people behind it. They foster growth, fairness, and stronger performance by anchoring ratings in clarity and courage. When bias is acknowledged and managed, leadership gains strength, credibility, and purpose.

"Leadership is not about eliminating bias—it is about illuminating it, owning it, and choosing fairness anyway." — Dr. Patrick C. Patrong.

Conducting Effective Evaluation Conversations

A performance evaluation is more than a document—it is a dialogue. It is the moment when a year's worth of observations, experiences, and outcomes are distilled into a conversation that can inspire clarity, confidence, and commitment. However, for many supervisors in the public sector, this moment brings anxiety, awkwardness, or avoidance.

This chapter provides practical guidance for preparing, delivering, and navigating evaluation conversations with intention and integrity. Whether affirming excellence or addressing gaps, how you communicate determines what the evaluation achieves. Done well, it strengthens trust and drives improvement. Done poorly, it sows confusion or disengagement. Let this chapter guide you toward confident, effective evaluation conversations—rooted in leadership, not just logistics.

What You Will Learn

- How to prepare for and structure an evaluation conversation with purpose and clarity.

- Ways to frame feedback that encourage accountability, learning, and development.

- Sample scripts by rating category to support confident and balanced delivery.

- Techniques to handle disagreement and complex responses professionally.

Preparing for the Discussion

Effective evaluation conversations begin long before the meeting. Preparation is not only about gathering notes—it is about building confidence, clarity, and readiness to lead. Supervisors must enter the conversation knowing what they want to communicate, why it matters, and how to express it clearly and respectfully.

Start by reviewing the employee's performance through the lens of the entire cycle, not just recent events. Identify patterns, strengths, gaps, and contributions. Make sure documentation supports each rating. When possible, include notes from prior check-ins, completed goals, peer feedback, and observations from multiple projects.

Next, organize your feedback around the evaluation's key competencies and goals. Consider where the employee falls on the five-point scale and prepare concrete examples to support your rating. Anticipate how the employee may respond—particularly to feedback that differs from their self-perception.

Select a quiet, neutral setting and schedule sufficient time for the conversation. Ensure privacy and avoid multitasking. The evaluation conversation should reflect the value you place on the employee's contribution.

Finally, enter the meeting with a developmental mindset. Evaluation should not be a verdict—it should be a dialogue. Aim to affirm strengths, provide clarity, and explore next steps for growth together.

Framing Feedback for Growth

The goal of feedback is not just to inform—it is to develop. How feedback is delivered determines how it is received. Even accurate feedback can fall flat if it is vague, accusatory, or disconnected from future improvement.

Growth-oriented feedback balances honesty with support. Begin by affirming strengths and contributions. From there, describe areas for growth using behavioral language—not personal judgments. Speak to the impact of actions, not intentions or attitudes.

Use the SBI model (Situation-Behavior-Impact) to guide your phrasing: "In the weekly reports (situation), your summaries were often delayed (behavior), which affected the team's ability to finalize data on time (impact)." This structure keeps the conversation factual, constructive, and less likely to trigger defensiveness.

Make space for two-way dialogue. Ask for the employee's perspective: "How do you see this?" or "What support would help improve this area?" Active listening shows respect and often reveals unseen challenges or misalignments.

Feedback should close with action. Frame the next step: "Let us work on X over the next quarter," or "I would like to see improvement in this area by your mid-year check-in." When feedback is framed as an invitation to grow, accountability becomes partnership.

Scripts by Rating Category

Supervisors often struggle to find the right words to convey different ratings. Below are sample phrases to support the delivery of evaluation across the five-point scale.

- **Extraordinary**: "Your leadership on the grant project did not just meet expectations—it reshaped how we approach funding. The results you achieved this year are not only exemplary, they have set a new benchmark for excellence."

- **Highly Successful**: "You consistently exceeded expectations, especially in the quality and reliability of your deliverables. Your initiative helped the team meet several tight deadlines, and your input improved our onboarding process significantly."

- **Successful**: "You met expectations this year with steady, consistent performance. Your work supported team goals and aligned well with your role. I appreciate your reliability and attention to your responsibilities."

- **Partially Successful**: "There were several contributions this year that met our expectations, but there were also instances— particularly in follow-up and responsiveness—where improvement is needed. I want to support you in building consistency moving forward."

- **Unsuccessful**: "Unfortunately, your performance this year did not meet the core expectations in several areas. These issues impacted your assignments and the team. Moving forward, we need to work together on a structured improvement plan."

Handling Disagreements and Difficult Moments

Not every evaluation conversation will be smooth. Sometimes employees are surprised, defensive, or discouraged. Supervisors must be prepared to hold the space with professionalism, empathy, and resolve.

Start by separating emotion from data. If an employee challenges a rating, ask clarifying questions to ensure a thorough understanding of the issue. "Can you help me understand what part you see differently?" Invite perspective, but stay anchored in evidence.

Listen attentively, but avoid backtracking from a fair and documented rating. Changing a rating out of discomfort undermines the process and creates inconsistencies. Let the employee know that their voice matters—and their feedback will be taken into account.

If an employee becomes emotional, pause to acknowledge: "I can see this is frustrating. That is okay—we can talk through it." Use calm body language and tone to help de-escalate the situation. Sometimes, a second conversation is necessary after the initial response has been made.

Remember: a difficult moment handled well builds trust. Employees do not need perfect ratings—they need fair ones. Furthermore, they need to know their supervisor can hold honest conversations with care and courage.

In Practice: Public Sector Case Snapshot

Diego, a program supervisor at a state workforce development agency, prepared to deliver a "Partially Successful" rating to Kendra, an analyst whose reporting accuracy had been inconsistent. Though he had documented missed deadlines and coaching conversations throughout the year, Diego dreaded the evaluation meeting. He softened the language and ultimately assigned her a "Successful" rating to avoid conflict.

Weeks later, a high-profile error in Kendra's report led to public scrutiny and internal fallout. Leadership questioned why a documented performance issue had not been addressed in her review. Diego admitted he had feared damaging the working relationship. What began as conflict avoidance led to organizational consequences—reminding Diego that difficult conversations are often the most essential.

Reflection Questions

- How do I prepare myself emotionally and mentally for performance conversations?

- Do I tend to soften ratings or feedback to avoid discomfort?

- What structures do I have in place to support fairness and consistency in conversations?

- Am I giving employees enough time to share their perspective during evaluations?

- What can I do to make evaluation conversations more developmental and less transactional?

In Practice: Key Takeaways

- Effective evaluation conversations are grounded in preparation, clarity, and developmental intent.

- Feedback should focus on behavior and impact, rather than personality or assumptions.

- Using scripts by rating category helps supervisors communicate with confidence and consistency.

- Difficult conversations are not failures—they are leadership moments that build trust.

- Dialogue, not monologue, transforms evaluations into tools for engagement and growth.

Leadership-Centered Summary

Evaluation conversations are where supervision becomes leadership. They reveal how clearly we see our teams, how honestly we communicate, and how courageously we lead when approached with empathy, structure, and the intent to build—not just judge—these conversations become more than compliance tools, they become culture-building moments.

Supervisors who lead these discussions with courage create clarity. Those who pair that clarity with care create trust. Furthermore, in public service, trust is the foundation of team resilience, engagement, and progress.

"An evaluation conversation is not a formality—it is a form of leadership. Done right, it changes how people see their work, their worth, and their way forward." — Dr. Patrick C. Patrong.

Tools for Supervisory Success

Supervisory success in the performance evaluation process depends on more than insight and intention—it requires tools that translate judgment into action. This chapter equips public sector supervisors with four essential tools to elevate evaluation practices and ensure fairness, consistency, and clarity across time. From visual frameworks to quick-reference checklists, these resources help supervisors document what matters, when it matters. Effective supervisors do not wait until evaluation season—they build a system for recognizing performance throughout the year. These tools will help you do exactly that.

What You Will Learn

- Understand the purpose and structure of the visual rating continuum.

- Use reflection prompts and evidence checklists to support fair and consistent evaluations.

- Apply a supervisor's quick reference guide during conversations and documentation.

- Develop habits for documenting feedback throughout the performance cycle.

The Visual Rating Continuum

Many supervisors find it difficult to explain the difference between a "Highly Successful" and an "Extraordinary" employee—or to defend why one person receives a lower rating than another. The Visual Rating Continuum offers a solution. It is a framework that helps clarify what each rating level looks like in practice, using language that is observable, measurable, and comparable.

This visual tool breaks down each of the five performance levels into plain-language behaviors. It highlights differentiators across levels and enables supervisors to connect ratings to specific examples, rather than relying on impressions. It also helps guide conversations, particularly when ratings may feel subjective to employees.

For example, a supervisor might say, "Your performance was Highly Successful because you proactively solved problems and exceeded your goals, but we reserve Extraordinary for those who have a transformative, sustained impact across the team." This process creates transparency and trust.

The Visual Rating Continuum is most effective when used not only at the end of the year, but throughout the entire performance cycle. Supervisors can refer to it during check-ins, progress reviews, and coaching conversations to help anchor expectations and ensure consistency.

Ultimately, the continuum is more than a graphic—it is a bridge between values and ratings. It reminds supervisors that performance levels should reflect patterns, not moments, and impact—not personality.

Reflection Prompts and Evidence Checklists

Supervisors often struggle with performance conversations because they lack concrete examples or clarity on how they arrived at a rating. Reflection prompts and evidence checklists serve as the internal guide before the evaluation form is ever completed.

Reflection prompts help supervisors ask the right questions: What did this employee improve this year? Where did they demonstrate initiative? How did their work impact the team, department, or public? These questions lead supervisors beyond generic praise or critique and into meaningful assessment.

Evidence checklists support consistency. By listing types of acceptable documentation—like project completion records, peer feedback, attendance logs, and coaching notes—these checklists help balance ratings with facts. They also prevent overreliance on recent memory or emotion.

Together, these tools create an evaluation ecosystem where every rating is backed by reflection and reinforced by evidence. They turn intuition into intention and provide a defense against bias.

A supervisor with good instincts may earn respect, but a supervisor with good tools earns credibility—and improves team trust in the process.

Quick Reference Guide

When delivering feedback or documenting performance, supervisors often lack the time to reference comprehensive training manuals. The Quick Reference Guide offers streamlined phrases, question prompts, and key behaviors aligned to each rating category.

This tool acts as a conversation coach. For example, under "Partially Successful," the guide might include phrases like, "There were successes, but consistency and follow-through are still developing," or "Let us build a plan to increase dependability going forward."

It also includes reminders about common rating pitfalls—such as the Shine Effect or Flash Effect—and offers sentence starters that help supervisors navigate difficult moments with poise and professionalism.

Because it is compact, the guide can be kept in a supervisor's desk, shared at team meetings, or used during peer calibration exercises. Its goal is not to replace judgment—but to support it with language and structure.

Think of it as a pocket-sized coach, ready to help you lead with clarity when the moment calls for it most.

Documenting Feedback Year-Round

Perhaps the most important supervisory habit in the evaluation process is year-round documentation. Too often, ratings are based on impressions or recent memory. This practice invites bias and weakens accountability.

Documenting performance does not require elaborate systems. A simple spreadsheet, running email folder, or notebook can track key contributions, setbacks, and coaching moments. These notes create a narrative of performance that supports a fair, accurate evaluation at year-end.

Mid-year check-ins are ideal checkpoints. Use them to verify whether goals are on track and note progress in each competency area. Documentation should be specific, factual, and time-stamped. Avoid over-documenting negatives—positive reinforcement should also be noted and shared regularly.

Encouraging employees to track their own contributions adds another layer of accountability. When employees come prepared with examples, supervisors gain new insight and ensure the evaluation reflects shared understanding.

Documentation is not bureaucracy—it is a matter of equity. It ensures that every rating reflects a complete picture, not a filtered one. Moreover, it gives supervisors the confidence to evaluate fairly, not with fear.

In Practice: Public Sector Case Snapshot

Janice, a frontline supervisor in the Department of Environmental Services, was known for her strong leadership but struggled with the documentation side of evaluations. She prided herself on knowing her team well and often relied on her memory when preparing performance reviews. This practice worked well for some employees, but when one of her team members, Aliyah, challenged a "Successful" rating, Janice could not produce concrete examples to justify her decision. Aliyah had kept her own records and presented a compelling case for a higher rating.

The incident caused tension, and HR recommended a recalibration process. Janice realized that relying solely on her instincts was not enough—credibility required structure. She began using a reflection checklist and a digital journal to document the highlights and challenges she encountered throughout the year. The following cycle, she delivered evaluations with more confidence, fewer disputes, and greater transparency.

Reflection Questions

- Do I have a reliable process for documenting employee performance throughout the year?

- Which evaluation tools am I currently using well, and which could I implement more consistently?

- How often do I refer to evidence or written examples when rating employee performance?

- Would my evaluation ratings withstand scrutiny by HR or a review committee?

- How can I use quick reference tools to strengthen conversations during reviews?

In Practice: Key Takeaways

- Tools like the Visual Rating Continuum and Quick Reference Guide help supervisors evaluate with clarity and confidence.

- Reflection prompts and evidence checklists support fair and balanced ratings grounded in documentation.

- Year-round feedback tracking reduces bias and builds credibility during evaluation discussions.

- Evaluation tools are not forms—they are frameworks for fairness, accountability, and growth.

- Supervisory success is not only about judgment—it is about preparation, clarity, and process.

Leadership-Centered Summary

Great leaders do not rely on guesswork. They build systems that help them see clearly, decide fairly, and lead consistently. The tools outlined in this chapter are not accessories—they are essentials. They help supervisors shift from instinct to evidence, from reaction to preparation. They elevate not just performance evaluations, but the daily habits that drive team development.

When public sector supervisors embrace these tools, they move from paperwork to purpose. They create evaluations that are not only accurate but also transformative.

"Supervision becomes leadership when instinct is paired with evidence—and tools turn insight into action." — Dr. Patrick C. Patrong.

Case Studies in Application

The most powerful lessons in performance evaluation do not come from theory—they come from experience. This chapter presents real-world case studies from public sector environments that illustrate how evaluation practices—when used effectively or ineffectively—can shape outcomes, morale, and leadership credibility. Each scenario reveals common challenges and practical takeaways for supervisors. Whether you have struggled with rating inflation, avoided difficult feedback, or led a successful turnaround, these examples will deepen your insight and sharpen your evaluative instincts.

What You Will Learn

- Recognize the impact of inflated ratings on performance culture and accountability.

- Understand how overuse of "Successful" ratings affects motivation and retention.

- Learn how coaching conversations can significantly impact your performance trajectory.

- Explore how consistent, fair evaluation practices shape team trust and performance.

Inflated Ratings and Their Consequences

In a midsize city health department, a supervisor named Olivia consistently rated her team as "Highly Successful" or "Extraordinary," even when their performance did not meet the criteria. She believed generous ratings would motivate employees and preserve harmony.

Over time, this strategy backfired. High performers felt their work was not meaningfully distinguished. Underperformers assumed they were exceeding expectations. When the department implemented a new bonus system linked to ratings, trust collapsed—many questioned how ratings were determined.

HR conducted an audit and found wide inconsistencies. Olivia had no supporting documentation for the inflated ratings. Her credibility suffered, and she lost her role as evaluation lead.

Inflated ratings feel good in the moment—but they damage long-term fairness and engagement. Employees want recognition, but they also want standards they can trust. Supervisors must rate performance truthfully, supported by evidence, and differentiate contributions with intention. Integrity in ratings protects the team and the leader.

The Cost of Rating Everyone "Successful"

At a public utility agency, all 20 team members in one division had received "Successful" ratings for three years in a row. Supervisors justified this with phrases like, "We are all doing our jobs," or "No one is causing problems."

However, during an internal promotion process, leaders struggled to identify top candidates. Without differentiated evaluations, everyone looked the same on paper—even those who had gone above and beyond.

Employees began to question the value of the evaluation process. "Why try harder if we are all rated the same?" one technician asked. Engagement dropped, and two top performers left for other departments.

Leadership responded by training supervisors on how to use the five-point scale. Within a year, ratings were more balanced—and performance conversations became more honest and productive.

Uniform ratings may feel safe, but they erode motivation and cloud succession planning. Evaluation must reflect not just participation, but contribution and growth.

A Turnaround through Coaching

Keisha, a housing authority supervisor, had a team member named Marcus who routinely missed deadlines and avoided collaboration. For two years, his evaluations noted "Partially Successful" performance with slight improvement. Rather than repeat the same process, Keisha changed her approach. She began monthly coaching sessions with Marcus, using a structured feedback template and development goals.

At first, Marcus resisted. However, after two consistent months of focused support, his participation improved. He met his first quarterly goal and began volunteering for new assignments. By the following annual review, Marcus had earned a "Successful" rating. His morale had improved, and he credited the turnaround to "finally being seen and supported."

This case shows that evaluation does not end with the form—it begins with the follow-through. Coaching, when intentional and sustained, can shift even long-standing patterns.

Building a Culture of Accountability

A regional transportation authority committed to improving performance outcomes after several audits revealed poor service response and documentation gaps. New leadership implemented a revised evaluation framework and trained supervisors to rate with fairness and rigor. At first, many feared backlash from shifting from years of leniency.

Nevertheless, when applied consistently, the new approach empowered teams to discuss expectations openly and transparently. Ratings varied more widely, but feedback became more constructive. Supervisors reported more meaningful conversations and a clearer sense of standards. Within two years, service delivery improved, employee satisfaction scores rose, and a sense of pride returned to the organization.

A culture of accountability does not come from top-down mandates—it has been built from everyday evaluation moments, where truth and trust meet.

In Practice: Public Sector Case Snapshot

Tanisha, a program manager at a youth services agency, noticed that performance conversations often stalled because supervisors lacked real examples. She piloted a new practice: supervisors collected highlights, concerns, and coaching notes in a shared folder after each project. Within six months, evaluations became more specific, more defensible, and more impactful. The initiative was later adopted agency-wide. One small system change elevated the entire performance culture.

Reflection Questions

- Have I ever inflated a rating to avoid conflict or reward effort over outcomes?

- How do I differentiate between meeting expectations and exceeding them in evaluations?

- What systems do I have in place to support year-round documentation of performance?

- When have I seen coaching make a difference—and how can I use it more intentionally?

- What would it take to shift my team's culture toward greater accountability and clarity?

In Practice: Key Takeaways

Inflated or uniform ratings may feel easier—but they harm fairness and credibility.

Differentiated evaluations strengthen succession planning and employee engagement.

Coaching can transform underperformance—when done consistently and constructively.

- Evaluation conversations are opportunities to affirm, redirect, and recalibrate.

- A culture of accountability grows through daily feedback, honest ratings, and leadership modeling.

Leadership-Centered Summary

Supervisors shape evaluation culture every time they rate performance, provide feedback, or lead development conversations. Case studies are not just examples—they are mirrors, reflecting what is possible and what must change. From inflated ratings to transformative coaching, the common thread is leadership—the choice to evaluate with integrity and invest in others.

If we want a better public sector, we must build better evaluation habits. Every form, every conversation, every rating is an opportunity to shape a stronger future.

"Every evaluation you complete is a cultural blueprint—it tells your team what you truly value, expect, and believe is possible." — Dr. Patrick C. Patrong.

Sustaining a Culture of Performance

Evaluating well once is commendable. Nevertheless, building a culture where performance conversations are ongoing, honest, and expected—that is leadership. In this final chapter, we turn to sustaining a high-performance culture. Supervisors play a critical role in reinforcing standards, modeling fairness, and connecting evaluations to organizational development. When evaluations are integrated into daily leadership practices, they shift from moments of judgment to moments of alignment. This chapter examines the essential elements of normalizing evaluative courage, calibrating across teams, developing internal talent, and continually growing as a supervisor in the public service sector.

What You Will Learn

- How to normalize honest feedback and evaluative courage across your team.

- Why Calibration Strengthens Fairness and Improves Organizational Consistency.

- Ways to Link Evaluations to Succession Planning and Talent Development.

- How to engage in continuous improvement as a supervisor and leader.

Normalizing Evaluative Courage

Evaluative courage is the willingness to give honest feedback, even when it is uncomfortable. It is a muscle that must be built through practice and reinforced through example.

Supervisors often default to vague ratings or soft language to avoid conflict. However, avoiding discomfort erodes trust, engagement, and accountability. Teams thrive when expectations are clear and feedback is direct and constructive. To normalize evaluative courage, leaders must reward it—not punish it. Supervisors who take a stand for clarity and fairness should be supported, not second-guessed.

One way to promote this mindset is through coaching circles, where supervisors can practice giving feedback and calibrate language before formal reviews.

Evaluative courage does not mean being harsh—it means being truthful. Moreover, in the public sector, where transparency and equity are deeply valued, that truth is not optional—it is essential.

Team Calibration and Equity

Calibration is the process of aligning evaluation standards across a unit or organization to ensure fairness and consistency in assessment. Without it, performance reviews can vary widely based on the supervisor's style, bias, or comfort level.

Team calibration sessions enable supervisors to discuss example ratings, share rationales, and address inconsistencies. These conversations foster learning, improve accountability, and reduce perceptions of favoritism.

Equity in evaluations is not about rating everyone the same—it is about ensuring that ratings reflect real contributions and are supported by consistent expectations and criteria.

Calibration also provides an opportunity to check for rating trends, identify bias patterns, and offer guidance to newer supervisors from more experienced peers. Organizations that value equity must invest in calibration. When teams align on how they rate performance, employees experience evaluations as fair, credible, and motivating.

Using Evaluations to Build Talent Pipelines

Evaluations are not just about the past—they are about the future. They are a powerful tool for identifying talent, shaping career paths, and building leadership pipelines.

Supervisors should use the evaluation process to spot potential, not just rate current output. Ask questions like: Who is ready to take on more responsibility? Who has demonstrated traits of future leadership?

Documenting potential is key. Utilize development goals and progress notes to monitor employee growth, identify strengths, and pinpoint areas for coaching. This data becomes invaluable in promotion and succession planning.

Link evaluations to training, mentorship, and stretch assignments. Let employees know that their performance review is also a career conversation—not just a scorecard.

In a high-performing culture, every evaluation is an opportunity to grow people, not just assess them. Moreover, every supervisor becomes a steward of the organization's future leaders.

Continuous Improvement in Supervisory Practice

Evaluation excellence does not happen by accident. It evolves through reflection, feedback, and practice. Supervisors must treat their own performance as an area for growth.

After each review cycle, reflect: What worked? What surprised me? Where did I hesitate—and why? These questions help build insight and intentionality over time.

Seek feedback from employees on the clarity and fairness of the evaluation conversation. Create space for honest dialogue—not to defend ratings, but to refine delivery.

Supervisors can also participate in peer coaching, review evaluation samples together, or join communities of practice focused on public sector performance leadership.

When supervisors model continuous improvement, they elevate the standard across the team. They show that growth is not just for staff—it is the mark of every committed leader.

In Practice: Public Sector Case Snapshot

Lamar, a district manager in a state licensing division, initiated quarterly calibration meetings with his supervisors after recognizing vast differences in how ratings were applied. He encouraged peer review, discussion of evidence, and shared evaluation language. Over time, rating accuracy improved, and employee satisfaction with the process increased. Lamar's initiative became a model across the department, proving that fairness is not accidental—it is a discipline built through shared practice.

Reflection Questions

- When have I avoided giving honest feedback due to fear of conflict or discomfort?

- How could team calibration improve fairness and consistency in my unit?

- How do I connect evaluations to development and career planning?

- What feedback have I received—or could I request—about my evaluation style?

- What one practice could I adopt this year to improve my own performance as a supervisor?

In Practice: Key Takeaways

- Evaluative courage creates clarity and builds trust across teams.

- Calibration ensures consistency and promotes equity in performance ratings.

- Evaluations should identify talent and align with long-term development planning.

- Supervisors must engage in continuous improvement to model excellence in leadership.

- Consistent habits—not occasional efforts —sustain cultural change.

Leadership-Centered Summary

A culture of performance is not built in a season—it is sustained through intention, repetition, and shared ownership. Supervisors are the culture carriers of public service. The way you evaluate, coach, and invest in your people tells them what leadership looks like and what excellence means.

When evaluation becomes part of your daily leadership rhythm— not just an annual obligation—you build something enduring. You do not just complete reviews—you elevate the culture.

"Sustaining a culture of performance is not about what you do once a year—it is about how you lead every day." — Dr. Patrick C. Patrong.

Writing Effective Evaluation Comments

Words shape perception. Nowhere is this truer than in performance evaluations. The comments supervisors and employees write can either illuminate growth or obscure it in vague, recycled phrases. Effective comments bridge intention and impact—they show that the process is about development, not documentation. This chapter teaches supervisors and employees how to craft comments that clarify expectations, highlight accomplishments, and direct future performance. The goal is not just to write well, but to write meaningfully.

What You Will Learn

- • How supervisors can write comments that guide performance improvement with clarity and evidence.

- • How employees can write self-assessment comments that reflect ownership, growth, and accountability.

- • Common mistakes to avoid when writing evaluation remarks.

- • Sample language that demonstrates action, behavior, and measurable outcomes.

For Supervisors — Writing with Clarity and Purpose

Comments transform numbers into narratives. A rating alone says what—but a comment explains why. Well-written comments strengthen fairness, transparency, and trust. They demonstrate that supervisors have observed, documented, and understood performance throughout the year.

Weak comments like "Good job overall" or "Needs improvement" say nothing about behavior or future expectations. Strong comments tie performance to evidence and outline specific steps for continued success or correction.

Principles for Effective Supervisor Comments

- • Be Specific and Evidence-Based: Avoid generalities. Instead of "Dependable worker," write: "Completed all quarterly reports on time with a 98% accuracy rate, ensuring deadlines were consistently met despite staffing shortages."

- • Connect to Agency Goals: Show how the employee's work supports broader priorities: "Your coordination of the recycling outreach campaign directly supported our department's goal of increasing public engagement by 15% this year."

- • Balance Recognition with Direction: Every comment should affirm what works and clarify what comes next.

- • Describe Observable Actions, Not Personal Traits: Replace adjectives with behaviors, e.g., avoid "Unmotivated," write: "Missed three follow-up deadlines despite reminders, which delayed project completion."

- • Include Forward-Focused Development Goals: Each improvement comment should show the employee how to improve, not just that improvement is needed.

Sample Supervisor Comment Framework (SBI + growth)

Extraordinary: During the March policy rollout, you anticipated stakeholder concerns and created a clarifying guide, which resulted in a 40% reduction in staff inquiries. Continue expanding your influence by mentoring others on proactive communication strategies.

Highly Successful: You consistently identified process improvements, such as the new ticket-tracking system, which enhanced service delivery time by 20%. To reach "Extraordinary," consider leading a cross-department initiative to share best practices.

Successful: You met project deadlines and maintained compliance with all reporting requirements. Over the next year, focus on enhancing collaboration by initiating monthly check-ins with partner teams to foster open communication and mutual understanding.

Partially Successful: Missed two of five data submission deadlines, causing delays in budget reconciliation. To progress to "Successful," establish a tracking calendar and submit draft reports for review two days before due dates.

Unsuccessful: Did not complete assigned policy updates despite multiple check-ins, resulting in operational gaps. Immediate improvement is required—complete outstanding items within 30 days and meet weekly with your supervisor for progress monitoring.

For Employees — Writing Self-Assessment Comments

An evaluation is incomplete without the employee's perspective. Self-assessment comments help employees reflect on progress, clarify challenges, and propose development goals. They also provide context that the supervisor may not have seen—such as behind-the-scenes problem-solving or unrecognized contributions.

• Use "I" Statements with Evidence: "I developed a new tracking template that reduced errors by 15%. Not 'Did a good job keeping reports accurate.'"

- • Highlight Accomplishments, Not Activities: Activities describe effort; accomplishments describe impact.

- • Acknowledge Challenges Honestly: Demonstrate self-awareness and identify improvement steps.

- • Connect Efforts to Goals: Link actions directly to the agency's objectives.

- • Include Learning and Growth Goals: End each comment with a development plan or next-step action.

Reflection Questions for Employees

- • What are the three most significant accomplishments I achieved this year?

- • Where did I experience the most growth?

- • What challenges hindered my progress—and what support would help overcome them?

- • How do my goals align with the organization's mission?

Leadership-Centered Closing Summary

Writing evaluation comments is an act of leadership. It requires observation, honesty, and a shared commitment to growth. Supervisors who provide clear, evidence-based comments empower employees to improve with direction—not confusion. Employees who write thoughtful self-assessments show maturity, engagement, and readiness to grow. Together, these voices create a culture where performance is not just recorded, but elevated.

"Clarity in writing breeds clarity in performance. Every comment is a bridge between what is and what could be." — Dr. Patrick C. Patrong.

Conclusion: Elevate Culture, One Conversation at a Time

Performance evaluation in the public sector is more than a requirement—it is a cultural signal. It tells employees what is valued, what is possible, and what leadership looks like in action. Throughout this book, we have explored the mechanics and mindset behind practical evaluation. We have examined tools, addressed bias, and walked through conversations that define and shape careers.

At the heart of it all is a simple belief: evaluation is leadership. It requires courage to provide honest feedback, clarity to define performance, consistency to ensure fairness, and compassion to develop people. It is not merely about completing a form—it is about laying the foundation for a performance culture built on trust, accountability, and growth.

This conclusion expands that belief into daily leadership practice—one built through ongoing feedback, meaningful conversations, and performance planning that keeps growth alive throughout the year.

What You Will Learn

• **How ongoing feedback shapes performance and trust.**

• **How to balance formal and informal conversations for lasting impact.**

• **How performance planning connects daily work to long-term results.**

• **How to build a feedback-ready culture that values clarity and development.**

The Power of Ongoing Feedback

Great organizations are not defined by what happens once a year—they are determined by what happens every day. Ongoing feedback transforms supervision into a partnership. It helps employees understand expectations in real time, not retroactively. When feedback is frequent, specific, and respectful, it eliminates surprises and builds confidence.

Feedback should be viewed as a continuous exchange: recognizing what is working well and providing guidance on areas for improvement. Supervisors who provide consistent feedback demonstrate that they are invested in their team's success. Employees respond with greater engagement, ownership, and initiative.

Effective feedback is not about catching mistakes—it is about cultivating awareness. A short note after a presentation or a comment after a project update can be as powerful as a formal evaluation if it reinforces growth and accountability.

Formal and Informal Conversations

Feedback takes many forms. Formal conversations occur during planned evaluations, progress reviews, or mid-year check-ins. Informal conversations occur in real-time, such as after a meeting, during a site visit, or in a hallway discussion. They are essential to sustaining performance dialogue.

Formal conversations provide structure and documentation, ensuring transparency and fairness. Informal conversations foster connection and immediacy, demonstrating that feedback is an integral part of everyday culture rather than an annual event. Consider the examples below:

Formal Feedback Example

- **Supervisor**: "In your quarterly report, your analysis was thorough and well-documented. One area for growth is timing—reports were submitted three days after the deadline. How can we adjust your workload or review schedule to help you remain on track?"

- **Employee**: "I appreciate that feedback. I have been splitting time across two projects. I will start scheduling report preparation earlier and review progress weekly."

Informal Feedback Example

- **Supervisor**: "I noticed how you handled that citizen inquiry today—excellent composure under pressure. That is the professionalism our team needs to model."

- **Employee**: "Thank you. It helped to remember our communication standards from training."

Formal conversations set the vision. Informal conversations reinforce it. Together, they create rhythm, credibility, and a sense of connection.

Performance Planning as a Leadership Discipline

Performance planning is not paperwork—it is purpose. A well-crafted plan links the employee's work to the agency's mission while identifying stretch goals that develop capability. Planning conversations must be collaborative. Supervisors should ask employees what success means to them, then align those responses with the organization's priorities.

A strong plan includes measurable objectives, resources for growth, and checkpoints for feedback. It also anticipates challenges, creating opportunities for proactive support rather than reactive correction. This transparency improves a shared responsibility.

Example: "Let us set a goal to reduce processing time by ten percent this quarter. What tools or workflow changes would help you achieve that?" By involving the employee in goal creation, the supervisor builds accountability through ownership.

Building a Feedback-Ready Culture

Creating a culture that fosters feedback requires intentional effort. Supervisors must model openness, humility, and responsiveness. When employees see leaders accept feedback themselves, they learn that feedback is not criticism—it is commitment to growth.

A feedback-ready culture is one where conversations are safe, timely, and two-way. Supervisors listen as much as they speak. Recognition is public when appropriate, correction is private, and growth is constant. The measure of leadership becomes not only how we evaluate others, but how we invite evaluation of ourselves.

In such an environment, evaluation is not a form; it is a rhythm. Conversations flow upward, downward, and across teams. Learning becomes the standard, and accountability becomes shared pride.

In Practice: Public Sector Case Snapshot

Marcus, a division manager at a regional planning office, inherited a team frustrated by years of unclear expectations. Annual evaluations were completed for compliance rather than conviction. Marcus introduced quarterly feedback sessions and encouraged supervisors to hold brief, informal check-ins every two weeks. Within six months, employee satisfaction scores increased by eighteen percent, and turnover decreased by half. The difference was not a new form—it was a new rhythm of conversation.

Reflection Questions

- • How often do I provide feedback that is specific and actionable?

- • Do my employees view evaluation as dialogue or documentation?

- • How can I use informal conversations to reinforce formal performance goals?

- • What systems can I create to maintain continuous feedback throughout the year?

- • How do I invite feedback on my own leadership performance?

Key Takeaways

- • Ongoing feedback sustains performance and builds trust.

- • Formal and informal conversations reinforce one another.

- • Performance planning links individual growth to organizational mission.

- • Leaders must normalize feedback to strengthen culture.

- • Evaluation excellence is a daily act, not an annual event.

Leadership-Centered Closing Summary

The actual test of leadership is not found in what is written on a form, but in what is spoken throughout the year. Every conversation—formal or spontaneous—has the power to build or diminish engagement. When supervisors choose to communicate with clarity and compassion, they transform evaluation into elevation.

Culture does not shift solely through policy. It evolves when leaders model what feedback looks like, sounds like, and feels like. Feedback becomes the heartbeat of leadership—the rhythm that keeps teams aligned, motivated, and focused on purpose.

"Every conversation is a chance to lead. Feedback is not a task—it is a tone that defines the culture you create." — Dr. Patrick C. Patrong.

About the Book

Evaluate to Elevate is a groundbreaking guide for public sector supervisors seeking to lead with clarity, courage, and impact. Combining real-world case studies, practical tools, and leadership insight, this book demystifies performance evaluations. It reframes them as one of the most powerful tools for developing people and building culture. Whether you are a new supervisor or a seasoned manager, this book offers a step-by-step roadmap for turning evaluations into lasting leadership moments.

About the Author

Dr. Patrick C. Patrong is a nationally recognized expert in organizational development, public sector oversight, and performance leadership. With over 30 years of experience in state and city agencies, he offers a practitioner's perspective on evaluation, grounded in academic rigor and executive coaching skills. Dr. Patrong is the President & CEO of Patrong Enterprises, Inc., a certified Lean Six Sigma Black Belt, and a dedicated advocate for equity, accountability, and excellence in public service.

www.ingramcontent.com/pod-product-compliance
Lightning Source LLC
Chambersburg PA
CBHW070012100426
42741CB00012B/3215